The Last Ride
of Wild Bill

Sterling A. Brown

The

LAST RIDE

of

WILD BILL

and Eleven Narrative Poems

bp

BROADSIDE PRESS

12651 Old Mill Place   Detroit, Michigan 48238

LCN: 73-83579
ISBN: 0-910296-01-4 cloth $6.00
ISBN: 0-910296-02-2 paper $3.00

Contents

Preface by Dudley Randall

April 18, 1973 was an important date for Broadside Press. That night some of us attending the Gwendolyn Brooks seminar at Howard University—Gwendolyn Brooks, the Carl Carters, Mari Evans, Hoyt Fuller, Don Lee, and I were invited to the Sterling Browns' home. There, we literally sat at the feet of the venerated poet while he showed us his rare books and entertained us with anecdotes ("lies," he called them) of W.E.B. DuBois, Walter White, and other outstanding men he had known.

His lovely and gracious wife, Daisy, plied us with tidbits and drinks, and made us feel comfortably at home, but we did little talking, for it was more enjoyable to listen to Sterling Brown. He had just returned from a successful poetry reading at an eastern college, and was in an exhilarated mood. Stories and witticisms poured from his lips. We thoroughly enjoyed his tall tales, and Daisy said that his talking with the younger poets was stimulating for him too. There was fine communication between three generations of poets: Brown representing the Negro Renaissance, Brooks and myself representing the post-Renaissance generation who had been nurtured by Brown and his contemporaries, and Lee, Evans, and Carter the new poets of the 1960's.

I had asked Brown several times to let Broadside Press publish his poems. His book *Southern Road* had been out of print for years. But he had never given me a definite answer. That night he announced definitely that Broadside Press would publish a book containing a collection of his ballads, including the Slim Greer series, the "Ballad of Joe Meek," and the unpublished long poem, "The Last Ride of Wild Bill."

Brown's one book of poetry, *Southern Road,* published in 1932, had been long out of print and was available only in libraries, although a number of his poems were reprinted in anthologies. I wanted this fine poet to be available again in collected form, so that readers could enjoy a whole book of his poems. I played a recording of Brown reading some of his poems to my class in Black Poetry, and although we had not had time to discuss his poems in class, the students enjoyed his strong, sensitive, earthy, humorous poetry so much that a large percentage of them wrote their papers on Sterling Brown.

Broadside Press is proud to make this book-length collection of Sterling Brown's poems available to readers. Perhaps Sterling Brown won't agree with me, for he points to many poems available in anthologies, but I believe it is necessary to keep a poet before the public in a *collection* of his poems, where readers can enjoy his full scope and variety. I am convinced that *The Last Ride of Wild Bill* will make many young readers aware of this eminent poet whose book has been so long out of print, and that a new generation will acclaim his poetry.

Dudley Randall
Detroit, 16 May 1974

The Last Ride of Wild Bill

I.

THE CHALLENGE

The new Chief of police
Banged his desk
Called in the force, and swore
That the number-running game was done
And Wild Bill
Would ride no more.

The rumor
Spread quickly
Caught up with Wild Bill,
In Darktown
At his rendezvous.
It left him untouched
Left him cool,
He went on shooting
His game of pool.
He ran up fifteen
And then he spat.
"Rack 'em up," he said.
His voice was flat.
He put a lead slug
In the telephone
He spoke to the Chief
In a tone
Colorless, sad,
As if what he had
To say was hurting him
Pretty bad.
"I just heard the news
You spread over town.

I raise you one,
I call your bluff.
Your cops
Are not quite tough
Enough.
And you ain't so smart,
I will be bound,
To run the
Great Wild Bill
To ground.
I'd like you to know,
What I thought you knew,
You have bit off more
Than you'll ever chew.
As long as loose change
Is in this town
Wild Bill
Will still
Run the numbers down."

2.
THE NEWS

The news flashed.
Messenger boys dashed,
Hither and yon,
Yon and hither.
The town was in one hell of a dither.
Big business got the jitters
Did the hootchie-kootchie
From Stone Mountain down
To the Chattahoochee
From Marietta,
To Decatur,
From the muckamucks
And the highty-tighty,

Down to the people on relief.
The talk was about
The Gawd-almighty
Brass-bound impudence
Of the Chief.

The slot machine boys
Deserted their slots;
The pool-room boys
Scratched their shots;
The beer-garden boys
Turned down their pots.
Even Madame Mamie
When she heard
Suspended business
Till further word.
Tailoring places
And beauty salons
Wondered how
They could carry on.
Till the Chamber of Commerce
Released a release:
"Wild Bill's stock
Is due to rise;
Carloading will increase
Likewise."

"Lay your money where your heart is,"
Said big business.

Confidence mounted
To the skies.

CIVIC RESPONSE

The folks responded with civic pride:
In North Side Drive,
On Ponce de Leon,
All over the city's
Ritzy side
Many a Dixie matron
And her scion
Wagered that Wild Bill
Still
Would ride.
In Pittsburgh section,
Beaver Slide,
Ward Eight, West End and
Summer Hill,
Side bets were made
And big dough laid
And the odds were heavy
On Wild Bill.
These were the people
That the bug had bit,
Betting now
On a sure-fire hit:
Kiwanians and Rotarians
Daughters, Sons, Cousins
Of Confederate Veterans,
The Kleagle of the Ku Klux Klan,
The Knights of the Pantry
And Dames of the Pan,
The aristocrats, the landed gentry,
The cracker, and the jigaboo
Hoi-polloi
All seemed to think well
Of their boy,

Were eager to lay
Their bucks on Bill.

On Druid Hill
An old-stock cavalier tried to bet
His yard-boy part of his back-pay due
But Mose he believed in Wild Bill too.
A U.D.C.
Gave five to three
To her three-in-one- mammy-laundress-cook,
Down at Five Points
They set up a scoreboard,
To tell folks the newest odds
On the book.
Money was talking
Five dollars to two
Said Wild Bill would bring
The numbers through.

4.
THE DAY: THE CHIEF

Into his office
The new Chief came
Not chipper, but game,
Not running away.
On his desk
A telegram lay:
"Ride my route
Again today;
Start at noon,
End at three.
Guess it will have
To be you and me."
The telegram was C.O.D.

The Chief's bald head
Flushed beet red.
His jaw clicked shut
On the masticated stogie butt.

The office was sinister
And still.
The new electric time piece ticked
Off the last few hours till
The Chief's appointment with Wild Bill.

The Chief was stumped
But he wasn't licked.
He watched the clock
Then something clicked.
"I got it," he said.
He fingered through the telephone book.
His breath came fast.
His fingers shook.
He talked to himself,
Nervous, grim,
"Since it will have to be
Me or him,
I choose him.
And him it will be
By hook or crook."
He took the telephone
Off the hook.

5.
THE DAY: WILD BILL

At eleven-thirty
Wild Bill was ready,
His voice was steady
But his temper dirty.
He got up from his business lunch.

They fixed him up
A Planter's Punch.

He looked at the cherry and the lime with scorn,
Threw the fruit mixture in the sink
"No salad for me,
When I drink I drink."
Got a two-by-four scantling for a bracer,
Drank a tumbler of corn
With rye for a chaser.
He looked at the clock,
Ten minutes to go.
He looked at his jumper
Who was looking low.
He said: "Today's run
May be tough.
Guess I'll make
My own jumps today."
The jumper spoke up
Quick and gruff:
"The hell you say
And the hell you will,
Reckon I'm sticking from now until."
Bill looked at the kid
And said "O.K."
At eleven forty-eight,
They walked out to the parked V 8
He waved to the gang
Gathered at the door
"Be back on the dot
At half past four."

He kicked his tires
And they were solid,
Looked at his gas gauge
Gas O.K.

He stepped on his starter,
It turned over easy.
Wild Bill and his rider
Were on their way.

6.
THE DAY: THE SPECTATORS

The schools might as well
Have declared holiday;
In gala array
With ribbons and banners,
Munching on peanuts
And bananas
The kids were out
Lining the route
That Wild Bill
Was known to ride;
Even the principals weren't inside.

From Oglethorpe, Emery, and Georgia Tech,
Spelman, Morehouse, and Morris Brown,
The collegians were on hand;
Each institute of learning
Had its band.
The one from Agnes Scott
Was particularly hot.
Cheerleaders pranced
And crowds snake-danced.
It was quite intellectual
And advanced.
Even the theologues
Came from Gammon
To see the Law
Give war
To Mammon.
The flocks

Of the Ebelezer A.M.E.
And the Holy Jumpers were side by side,
Forgetting their battles
To see Bill Ride.
The Canon and the Dean
Of the Diocese of Infinitesimal Believers
Were out in their swallowtails and beavers,
Bestowing their blessing
On the scene.

Banks were shut,
Stores
Closed doors,
The wheels of industry
Were still:
The city fathers' tribute
To Wild Bill.

7.
THE CHASE: FIRST PART

The hounds crossed a false trail
In West End,
They bayed long,
Loud and wrong:
The fox was elsewhere
Idling along.
But on Pearson Road
They struck the trace,
Right after Bill
Had left the place.
The scent was new,
Foolproof and true,
So they settled doggedly
To the chase.

The fox, he grinned
I

He thought his tricks
Could save him from
A tighter fix.

But the hunter who ran
At the head of the pack
Was a master trailer
From way back.
And once the real run
Was begun,
The fox knew it wasn't
Just for fun.
So he soared up the hill,
Roared down the vale,
With the hounds a-baying
On his trail,
A bit too close
Upon his tail.

The sound of the sirens
Long and loud
Reached all the way
To the gathered crowd
Anxious, ready.
From the steady
Resolute, collected baying
They knew the Chief's pack
Wasn't playing.

But still they knew
Their Wild Bill too.

8.
THE CHASE: SECOND PART

Up on Ashby
The cops were gaining

Wild Bill sure
Seemed out of luck,
When out from an alley
Sam Johnson backed
In the remnants of a
Punch-drunk truck.
It settled in the middle of the tracks,
Right in front of the police car.
"Sorry, cap'n, but I do declah,
Havin' a little trouble here
Wid my truck.
I believe to my soul
De clutch done stuck."
The Chief he fumed and the cop he swore,
Like Sam had never heard before,
But the stuck—
Clutch truck
Was there to stay.
And the fox
Was eight good blocks
Away.

When Bill turned off
Of West Fair
They thought they had got him bottled there
Slicker than slick.
The usual thoroughfare
Was blind.
A truck of bricks broadside before
Two runabouts behind.
But Bill wasn't born to die in a bottle,
Quicker than quick
He opened the throttle;
Spun into a yard at fifty-three,
Backed out at sixty-four
Threw her in first at seventy-five

And side-swiped the law.
He turned the nearest corner
With three wheels in the air
Then settled back into his speed
And got the hell
Away from there.

At Grady Square
Wild Bill's need was sore again,
So a veteran
Who had stayed in front
Of Sherman, marching to the sea,
Tottered out,
And sang about
The Dixie where he wished to be.
He soon collected a singing throng.

The police came up at the second verse,
Halted, saluted, uncovered, and stood
Like the others of that multitude,
Lifting their voices in the song,
Solemn, sad,
Their harmonizing wasn't bad.
And when
The hymn had got to the long amen,
Wild Bill's chances
Were all to the good.
He was four miles from
That neighborhood.
"Look away, look away,
Look away, Dixie Land!"

Another Negro
Down at Decatur,
Held up the chase
A little later.

Waved his arms
Like a semaphore
Went into a dance,
Flagged down the Law.

They pulled up murderous,
But they pulled up quick.
The fellow talked slow,
Meek and low:
"You see it's like dis,
My wife is sick
And when I heard de siren blow
I thought dat dis was de ambulance.
I wants to beg yo' pardon
In advance."
They cursed him fierce,
They wished him dead.
They bent a night-stick
On his head.
He needed the ambulance
Really then.
But Wild Bill had been saved
Again.

9.
THE CHASE: THIRD PART

The fox heard the dogs bay
Far away
They had lost the scent
And they were spent
Danger was past
And at long last
The fox could safely head
For his den.
Wild Bill had foiled
The Law again.

He eased up his foot
Let the engine dally
It purred along
Like Rudy Vallee;
He turned to his jumper
By his side.
The jumper was beaming
And his grin was wide.
They checked
The collect
And were satisfied.
They had picked up the bags
As per schedule:
Third Baptist Church,
The Vocational School,
The Registrar's office
At the City Jail,
Braxton Bragg's statue
On the horse's tail,
Behind a hedge on the Courthouse lawn,
The Parish-House of the Cathedral
Of Saint John
Who saw the holy number
And so on.

From Sub-Station Q
On Auburn Avenue
From Sub-Station L
On the Stone Mountain Road
From the office of the Emergency Relief—
"Ain't missed nary one,"
The jumper told his chief.
From the H L A, the C C C,
The I B W O Z E,
The branch of the N-Double O. C. P.
The A. S. F. and the D. C. V.

The K. K. K.
All were registered
O. K.

Then Bill saw a bag
In a new place.
He looked at his jumper
With doubt in his face.
"Must be a new agent
We ain't checked.
But the bag is fat
And it looks correct,
It's a territory
We don't know,
But we better make a clean sweep
As we go."
The jumper brought it to him
Laid it on his knee,
It was heavier than a bag
Had right to be.
Bill held it to his ear,
Heard something tick,
Then he understood
The Chief's last trick.
As he threw it from him,
He heard the roar;
And then the great Bill
Knew no more.

10.
THE LAST COLLECT

When he came to,
His bus was hitting,
Lickety-splitting,
Hell bent on wheels
Down a straight dark road;

Only one battered headlight glowed.
His jumper was missing
And so was his car.

He looked to the right,
It was black as tar.
Looked to the left,
Blacker there.
The wheel was clammy,
The air was damp.
"Don't know where I'm going
But I've sure come far,
This must be the swamp
Near Florida."
Suddenly,
A red light glowed,
Like the world on fire
Down the road.
He pushed the gas-knob to the floor;
Almost too late
Right in the front of him he saw
A gray wall rising with a narrow gate.
This was a section of his state
That Wild Bill
Had not seen before.
His car leapt towards it with a roar.

His hubcaps grazed
The big black gate;
He slowed the wheel,
The old V 8
Missed by a hair
A big black mastiff lying there.
Then he spied
A crowd ahead;
"It's my hips this time,"

Old Wild Bill said,
But he grabbed his brake,
Stopped on the dime;
The engine sputtered,
Shuddered,
Stuttered,
Died with a groan, a cough, and a shake.
Wild Bill looked
But he could not speak;
What he saw there
Left him weak.
Coming toward
His dead machine
Was the worst looking mob
He had ever seen.
Then he heard such
An ungodly yell,
He knew
At last
He had gone to Hell.

Wild Bill said,
"I will be damn.
Been asked here frequent,
And here I am."

The devils rushed at him
In a swarm,
And the cool
Wild Bill
Grew awful warm.
It looked like he'd
Broke up a meeting;
But this was the Convocation's
Greeting:
They climbed all over
His running board,

"Wild Bill, Wild Bill!"
  Their shouting roared
  And rang through all the streets of Hell:

"Give us the number,
  Wild Bill,
  Tell us
  What fell!"

He Was a Man

It wasn't about no woman,
  It wasn't about no rape,
He wasn't crazy, and he wasn't drunk,
  An' it wasn't no shooting scrape,
    He was a man, and they laid him down.

He wasn't no quarrelsome feller,
  And he let other folks alone,
But he took a life, as a man will do,
  In a fight for to save his own,
    He was a man, and they laid him down.

He worked on his little homeplace
  Down on the Eastern Shore;
He had his family, and he had his friends,
  And he didn't expect much more,
    He was a man, and they laid him down.

He wasn't nobody's great man,
  He wasn't nobody's good,
Was a po' boy tried to get from life
  What happiness he could,
    He was a man, and they laid him down.

He didn't abuse Tom Wickley,
  Said nothing when the white man curst,
But when Tom grabbed his gun, he pulled his own,
  And his bullet got there first,
    He was a man, and they laid him down.

Didn't catch him in no manhunt,
  But they took him from a hospital bed,
Stretched on his back in the nigger ward,
  With a bullet wound in his head,
    He was a man, and they laid him down.

It didn't come off at midnight
   Nor yet at the break of day,
It was in the broad noon daylight,
   When they put po' Will away,
     He was a man, and they laid him down.

Didn't take him to no swampland,
   Didn't take him to no woods,
Didn't hide themselves, didn't have no masks,
   Didn't wear no Ku Klux hoods,
     He was a man, and they laid him down.

They strung him up on Main Street,
   On a tree in the Court House Square,
And people came from miles around
   To enjoy a holiday there,
     He was a man, and they laid him down.

They hung him and they shot him,
   They piled packing cases around,
They burnt up Will's black body,
   'Cause he shot a white man down;
     "He was a man, and we'll lay him down."

It wasn't no solemn business,
   Was more like a barbecue,
The crackers yelled when the fire blazed,
   And the women and the children too—
     "He was a man, and we laid him down."

The Coroner and the Sheriff
   Said "Death by Hands Unknown."
The mob broke up by midnight,
   "Another uppity Nigger gone—
     He was a man, an' we laid him down."

Sam Yancey

The whites had taught him how to rip
   A Nordic belly with a thrust
Of bayonet, had taught him how
   To transmute Nordic flesh to dust.

And a surprising fact had made
   Belated impress on his mind:
That shrapnel bursts and poison gas
   Were inexplicably color blind.

He picked up, from the difficult
   But striking lessons of the war,
Some truths that he could not forget,
   Though inconceivable before.

And through the lengthy vigils, stuck
   In never-drying stinking mud,
He was held up by dreams of one
   Chockfull of laughter, hot of blood.

2

On the return Sam Yancey cheered
   The dirty steerage with his dance,
Hot-stepping boy! Soon he would see
   The girl who beat all girls in France.

He stopped buckdancing when he reached
   The shanties at his journey's end;
He found his sweetheart in the jail,
   And took white lightning for his friend.

One night the woman whose full voice
   Had chortled so, was put away
Into a narrow, gaping hole;
   Sam sat beside till break of day.

He had been told what man it was
    Whose child the girl had had to kill,
Who best knew why her laugh was dumb,
    Who best knew why her blood was still.

And he remembered France, and how
    A human life was dunghill cheap,
And so he sent a rich white man
    His woman's company to keep.

3

The mob was in fine fettle, yet
    The dogs were stupid-nosed, and day
Was far spent when the men drew round
    The scrawny woods where Yancey lay.

The oaken leaves drowsed prettily,
    The moon shone down benignly there;
And big Sam Yancey, King Buckdancer,
    Buckdanced on the midnight air.

Slim Greer

Listen to the tale
Of old Slim Greer,
Waitines' devil
Waitin' here;

Talkinges' guy
An' biggest liar,
With always a new lie
On the fire.

Tells a tale
Of Arkansaw
That keeps the kitchen
In a roar;

Tells in a long-drawled
Careless tone,
As solemn as a Baptist
Parson's moan:

How he in Arkansaw
Passed for white,
An' he no lighter
Than a dark midnight.

Found a nice white woman
At a dance,
Thought he was from Spain
Or else from France;

Nobody suspicioned
Ole Slim Greer's race
But a Hill Billy, always
Roun' the place,

Who called one day
On the trustful dame
An' found Slim comfy
When he came.

The whites lef' the parlor
All to Slim
Which didn't cut
No ice with him,

An' he started a tinklin'
Some mo'nful blues,
An' a-pattin' the time
With No. Fourteen shoes.

The cracker listened
An' then he spat
An' said, "No white man
Could play like that . . . "

The white jane ordered
The tattler out;
Then, female-like,
Began to doubt,

Crept into the parlor
Soft as you please
Where Slim was agitatin'
The ivories.

Heard Slim's music—
An' then, hot damn!
Shouted sharp—"Nigger!"
An' Slim said, "Ma'am?"

She screamed and the crackers
Swarmed up soon,
But found only echoes
Of his tune;

> 'Cause Slim had sold out
> With lightnin' speed;
> "Hope I may die, sir—
> Yes, indeed . . . "

Slim Lands a Job?

Poppa Greer happened
   Down Arkansaw way,
An' ast for a job
   At Big Pete's Cafe.

        Big Pete was a six foot
           Hard-boiled man
        Wid a forty-four dungeon
           In his han'.

"Nigger, kin you wait?"
   Is what Pete ast;
Slim says, "Cap'n
   I'm jes' too fast."

        Pete says, "Dat's what
           I wants to hire;
        I got a slow nigger
           I'm gonna fire—

Don't 'low no slow nigger
   Stay roun' hyeah,
I plugs 'em wid my dungeon!"
   An' Slim says "Yeah?"

        A noise rung out
           In rush a man
        Wid a tray on his head
           An' one on each han'

Wid de silver in his mouf
   An' de soup plates in his vest
Pullin' a red wagon
   Wid all de rest . . .

De man's said, "Dere's
  Dat slow coon now
  Dat wuthless lazy waiter!"
  An' Slim says, "How?"

An' Slim threw his gears in
  Put it in high,
An' kissed his hand to Arkansaw,
  Sweetheart . . . good-bye!

Slim in Atlanta

Down in Atlanta,
  De whitefolks got laws
For to keep all de niggers
  From laughin' outdoors.

      Hope to Gawd I may die
        If I ain't speakin' truth
      Make de niggers do deir laughin'
        In a telefoam booth.

Slim Greer hit de town
  An' de rebs got him told,—
"Dontcha laugh on de street,
  If you want to die old."

      Den dey showed him de booth,
        An' a hundred shines
      In front of it, waitin'
        In double lines.

Slim thought his sides
  Would bust in two,
Yelled, "Lookout, everybody,
  I'm coming through!"

      Pulled de other man out,
        An' bust in de box,
      An' laughed four hours
        By de Georgia clocks.

Den he peeked through de door,
  An' what did he see?
Three hundred niggers there
  In misery.—

Some holdin' deir sides,
    Some holdin' deir jaws,
To keep from breakin'
    De Georgia laws.

An' Slim gave a holler,
    An' started again;
An' from three hundred throats
    Come a moan of pain.

An' every time Slim
    Saw what was outside,
Got to whoopin' again
    Till he nearly died.

An' while de poor critters
    Was waitin' deir chance,
Slim laughed till dey sent
    Fo' de ambulance.

De state paid de railroad
    To take him away;
Den, things was as usural
    In Atlanta, Gee A.

Slim Hears "The Call"

Down at the barbershop
    Slim had the floor,
"Ain't never been so
    Far down before.

        "So ragged, I make a jaybird
            About to moult,
        Look like he got on gloves
            An' a overcoat.

"Got to walk backwards
    All de time
Jes' a-puttin' on front
    Wid a bare behime.

        "Been down to skin and bones
            Gittin' down to de gristle,
        So de call sounds louder
            Dan a factory whistle.

"Big holes is the onlies'
    Things in my pocket,
So bein' a bishop
    Is next on de docket.

        "Lawd, lawd, yas Lawd,
            I hears de call,
        An' I'll answer, good Lawd,
            Don't fret none atall.

"I heard it once
    An' I hears it again
Broadcast from the station
    W-I-N!

"Gonna be me a bishop
    That ain't no lie,
Get my cake down here,
    An' my pie in the sky.

II

        "Saw a buddy th' other day,
            Used to know him well
        Best coon-can player
            This side of hell.

"Had a voice as deep
    As a bellerin' bull,
Called hogs in a way
    Jes' beautiful.

        "Ran across him down
            In Caroline
        Folks interduced him
            As a 'great divine'.

"Had on a jimswinger
    Hangin' low,
An' a collar put on
    Hindparts befo'.

        "At first I jes' couldn't
            Fix his face,
        Then I remembered him dealin'
            In Shorty Joe's place.

" 'You got de advantage
    Of me, I fear—'
Then all of a sudden
    'My dear—Brother Greer!'

"He let out a roar
   An' grabbed my hand:
'Welcome, thou Pilgrim
   To our Pleasant Land!'

"Took me to a house
   Like de State Capitol:
'Jes' a shanty, not fit
   Fo' you, at all

      " 'Brother Greer, but if
         You'll stay wid me
      I'll try to make it up
         In hosspitality'.

"Called in his wife
   As purty as sin,
An' his secketary, twict
   As purty again.

      "When dey went out, he winked
         An' said—'Well, Slim?'
      An' he looked at me,
         An' I looked at him.

III

"Little fatter an' greasier
   Than when we had been
Side pardners together
   In de ways of sin.

      "Ran a great big school,
         Was de president,
      'Brother Greer, jus' see
         What de Lawd hath sent!'

"An' he de kind of guy
    Was sich a fool
Dey had to burn down de shack
    To get him out of school.

        "When de other pupils
            Was doin' history
        He was spellin' cat
            With a double p.

"Couldn't do no problems,
    But was pretty good
At beatin' out erasers
    An' bringin' in wood.

        "But he knew what side de bread
            You put de butter on,
        An' he could figger all right
            For number one.

"So here he was de head man
    Of de whole heap—
Wid dis solemn charge dat
    He had to keep:

        "A passel of Niggers
            From near an' far
        Bringin' in de sacred bucks
            Regular.

"Stayed wid him a while,
    Watched him do his stuff,
Wid a pint of good sense,
    An' a bushel of bluff.

"Begged fo' his dyin' school
       At de conference
Took up nine thousand dollars
       An' eighty cents.

"An' I swear, as sure
       As my name's Slim Greer,
He repohted to de school
       Sixteen dollars clear.

       " 'Expenses pretty high',
              He said with a frown.
       An' de conference held
              In de very next town!

"Ordered the convention
       To Los Angeles,
'Ain't no members out there',
       Said his enemies.

       " 'Dat's jes' de reason
              Why we gotta go,
       Gotta missionize de heathen
              On de Western Sho'.

" 'Furrin parts is callin','
       De Bishop says,
'Besides, I got a cravin'
       Fo' oranges.'

              "Filled a Pullman wid de delegates
                     He liked de best,
              An' took a private plane
                     Fo' de Golden West.

"Las' words he said
   As he rose in de air:
'Do lak me; take you' troubles
   To de Lord in prayer.

     " 'Brother Greer, do that,
       An' you will see,
      De Lawd'll be wid you,
       Like he's been wid me.'

IV

"I remembers his words
   Now de North Wind blows
Like de Memphis special
   Through my holy clothes.

     "Now dat thinkin' of ham an' eggs
      Makes me sick
      Got me a longin'
       Fo' de bishopric.

"I kin be a good bishop,
   I got de looks,
An' I ain't spoiled myself
   By readin' books.

     "Don't know so much
      'Bout de Holy Ghost,
      But I likes de long green
      Better'n most.

"I kin talk out dis worl'
   As you folks all know,
An' I'm good wid de women,
   Dey'll tell you so . . .

V

"An' I says to all de Bishops,
  What is hearin' my song—
Ef de cap fits you, brother,
  Put it on."

Slim in Hell

Slim Greer went to heaven;
    St. Peter said, "Slim,
You been a right good boy."
    An' he winked at him.

        "You been a travelin' rascal
            In yo' day.
        You kin roam once mo';
            Den you comes to stay.

"Put dese wings on yo' shoulders,
    An' save yo' feet."
Slim grin, and he speak up
    "Thankye, Pete."

        Den Peter say, "Go
            To Hell an' see,
        All dat is doing, and
            Report to me.

"Be sure to remember
    How everything go."
Slim say, "I be seein' yuh
    On de late watch, bo."

        Slim got to cavortin',
            Swell as you choose,
        Like Lindy in de "Spirit
            Of St. Louis Blues!"

He flew an' he flew,
    Till at last he hit
A hangar wid de sign readin'
    DIS IS IT.

Den he parked his wings,
An' strolled aroun'
Gettin' used to his feet
On de solid ground.

II

Big bloodhound came aroarin'
Like Niagry Falls,
Sicked on by white devils
In overhalls.

Now Slim warn't scared,
Cross my heart, it's a fac',
An' de dog went on a bayin'
Some po' devil's track.

Den Slim saw a mansion
An' walked right in;
De Devil looked up
Wid a sickly grin.

"Suttinly didn't look
Fo' you, Mr. Greer,
How it happen you comes
To visit here?"

Slim say—"Oh, jes' thought
I'd drap by a spell."
"Feel at home, seh, an' here's
De keys to hell."

Den he took Slim around
An' showed him people
Raisin' hell as high as
De First Church Steeple.

Lots of folks fightin'
  At de roulette wheel,
Like old Rampart Street,
  Or leastwise Beale.

Showed him bawdy houses
  An' cabarets,
Slim thought of New Orleans
  An' Memphis days.

    Each devil was busy
      Wid a devilish broad,
    An' Slim cried, "Lawdy,
      Lawd, Lawd, Lawd."

Took him in a room
  Where Slim see
De preacher wid a brownskin
  On each knee.

    Showed him giant stills,
      Going everywhere
    Wid a passel of devils,
      Stretched dead drunk there.

Den he took him to de furnace
  Dat some devils was firing,
Hot as hell, an' Slim start
  A mean presspirin';

    White devils wid pitchforks
      Threw black devils on,
    Slim thought he'd better
      Be gittin' along.

An' he say—"Dis makes
   Me think of home—
Vicksburg, Little Rock, Jackson,
   Waco, and Rome.

     Den de devil gave Slim
       De big Ha-Ha;
     An' turned into a cracker,
       Wid a sheriff's star.

Slim ran fo' his wings,
   Lit out from de groun'
Hauled it back to St. Peter,
   Safety boun'.

III

     St. Peter said, "Well,
       You got back quick.
     How's de devil? An' what's
       His latest trick?"

An' Slim say, "Peter,
   I really cain't tell,
De place was Dixie
   Dat I took for hell."

     Then Peter say, "You must
       Be crazy, I vow,
     Where'n hell dja think Hell *was,*
       Anyhow?

"Git on back to de yearth,
   Cause I got de fear,
You'se a leetle too dumb,
   Fo' to stay up here . . . "

Crispus Attucks McKoy

I sing of a hero,
Unsung, unrecorded,
Known by the name
Of Crispus Attucks McKoy,
Born, bred in Boston,
Stepson of Garvey,
Cousin of Trotter,
Godson of DuBois.

No monastic hairshirt
Stung flesh more bitterly
Than the white coat
In which he was arrayed;
But what was his agony
On entering the drawing-room
To hear a white woman
Say slowly, "One spade."

He threw up his job,
His scorn was sublime,
And he left the bridge party
Simply aghast;
Lo, see him striding
Out of the front door
A free man again
His infamy past.

Down at the Common,
The cradle of freedom,
Another shock nearly
Carried him away
Someone called out "Shine"
And he let loose a blue streak,
And the poor little bootblack
Slunk frightened away.

In a bakery window
He read with a glance
"Brown Betties for sale"
And his molars gnashed;
Up came the kerbstone,
Back went his trusty arm,
Swift was his gesture,
The plate glass was smashed.

On the sub, Crispus
Could have committed murder,
Mayhem and cannibalism,
When he heard a maid
Say to the cherub
Opposite to her,
"Come over here, darling,
Here's a little shade."

But down at the Gardens,
He knew was his refuge,
Recompense for insults,
Solace for grief,
A Negro battler,
Slugging Joe Johnson
Was fighting an Irishman
Battling Dan O'Keefe.

The garden was crammed,
Mickeys, Kikes, Bohunks,
Polacks and Dagoes,
All over the place,
Crispus strode in,
Regally, boldly,
The sole representative
Of his race.

The fight was even,
When Joey hit Dan,
The heart of Crispus
Shone with a steady glow,
When Dan hit Joey,
Crispus groaned "foul,"
"Oh the dirty low-down
So-and-so."

> In the tenth round,
> Dan got to swinging,
> Joey was dazed,
> And clinched and held,
> When suddenly,
> Right behind Crispus,
> "Kill the Nigger!"
> Somebody yelled.

Crispus got up
In all of his fury;
Lightning bolts zigzagged
Out of his eyes,
With a voice like thunder
He blurted his challenge,
"Will the bastard who said that
Please arise."

> Thirty-five thousand
> Nordics and Alpines,
> Hebrews and Gentiles,
> As one man arose,
> See how our hero,
> Armed with his noble cause,
> Armed with righteousness
> To battle goes.

43

They found an ankle in Dedham,
A thighbone in Maldon,
An elbow in Somerville,
Both nostrils in Lynn,
And on Boston Common
Lay one of his eyebrows,
The cap of his knee,
And a piece of his shin.

> Peabody Museum
> Has one of his eardrums;
> His sound heart was found
> In Lexington;
> But over the reaches
> From Cape Cod to Frisco
> The soul of our hero
> *Goes marching on . . .*

A Bad, Bad Man

Forget about your Jesse James,
    And Billy the Kid;
I'll tell you instead what
    A black boy did.

        John Bias was a squinchy runt,
           Four foot two,
        Married to a strapping broad.
        Big-legged Sue.

Another boy, Sam Johnson,
    Was getting lynched because
His black mule had bust
    A white man's jaws.

        The crackers gathered in the woods
           Early that night.
        Corn liquor in pop bottles
           Got 'em right.

They tied Sam Johnson to a tree,
    Threw liquor on the fire.
Like coal oil it made the flames
    Shoot higher.

        Then Johnny Bias rushed in
           Looking awful sore,
        Waving a great big
           Forty-four.

The doctor he fell sick,
    The preacher fell on his knees,
The kids fell bass ackwards
    From the trees.

And all the women scattered
　Right close behind the men;
Then brave Little Johnnie walked
　Out again.

The fire had burnt the ropes;
　Sam jumped up and was gone
Down the other road from what
　The mob was on.

　　The state troops cam a-troopin'
　　Three days late,
　　And stayed near twenty minutes to
　　Investigate.

The crackers spoke, from then on,
　Of the giant nigger,
Every day he grew a
　Little bigger.

　　Johnnie was told the next day
　　What he had done for Sam,
　　Scratched his head and said, "Well
　　I be dam!

"Never had no notion
　To save nobody's life,
I was only jes a-lookin'
　For my wife."

Break of Day

Big Jess fired on the Alabama Central,
Man in full, babe, man in full.
Been throwing on coal for Mister Murphy
From times way back, baby, times way back.

Big Jess had a pleasing woman, name of
    Mamie,
Sweet-hipted mama, sweet-hipted Mame;
Had a boy growing up for to be a fireman,
Just like his pa, baby, like his pa.

Out by the roundhouse Jess had his cabin,
Longside the tracks, babe, long the tracks,
Jess pulled the whistle when they high-
    balled past it
"I'm on my way, baby, on my way."

Crackers craved the job what Jess was hold-
    ing,
Times right tough, babe, times right tough,
Warned Jess to quit his job for a white man,
Jess he laughed, baby, he jes' laughed.

He picked up his lunch-box, kissed his
    sweet woman,
Sweet-hipted Mama, sweet-hipted Mame,
His son walked with him to the white-
    washed palings,
"Be seeing you soon, son, see you soon."

Mister Murphy let Big Jess talk on the whistle
"So long sugar baby, so long babe";
Train due back in the early morning
Breakfast time, baby, breakfast time.

Mob stopped the train crossing Black Bear
   Mountain
Shot rang out, babe, shot rang out.
They left Big Jess on the Black Bear Moun-
   tain,
Break of day, baby, break of day.

Sweet Mame sits rocking, waiting for the
   whistle
Long past due, babe, long past due.
The grits are cold, and the coffee's boiled
   over,
But Jess done gone, baby; he done gone.

The Ballad of Joe Meek

I

You cain't never tell
  How far a frog will jump,
When you jes' see him planted
  On his big broad rump.

      Nor what a monkey's thinking
        By the working of his jaws—
      You jes' cain't figger;
        And I knows, because

Had me a buddy,
  Soft as pie
Joe Meek they called him
  And they didn't lie.

      The good book say
        "Turn the other cheek,"
      But that warn't no turning
        To my boy Joe Meek.

He turned up all parts,
  And baigged you to spank,
Pulled down his breeches,
  And supplied the plank.

      The worm that didn't turn
        Was a rattlesnake to Joe:
      Wasn't scary—jes' meek, suh,
        Was made up so.

49

It was late in August
  What dey calls dog days,
Made even beetle hounds
  Git bulldog ways.

      Would make a pet bunny
        Chase a bad blood-hound
      Make a new-born baby
        Slap his grandpa down.

The air it was muggy
  And heavy with heat,
The people all sizzled
  Like frying meat.

      The icehouse was heaven
        The pavements was hell
      Even Joe didn't feel
        So agreeable.

Strolling down Claiborne
  In the wrong end of town
Joe saw two policemen
  Knock a po' gal down.

      He didn't know her at all,
        Never saw her befo',
      But that didn't make no difference,
        To my ole boy Joe.

Walks up to the cops,
  And, very polite,
Ast them ef they thought
  They had done *just right*.

      One cracked him with his billy
        Above the left eye,

One thugged him with his pistol
And let him lie.

III

When he woke up, and knew
  What the cops had done,
Went to a hockshop,
  Got hisself a gun.

    Felt mo' out of sorts
      Than every befo',
    So he went on a rampage
      My ole boy Joe.

Shot his way to the station house.
  Rushed right in,
Wasn't nothing but space
  Where the cops had been.

    They called the reserves,
      And the national guard,
    Joe was in a cell
      Overlooking the yard.

The machine guns sputtered,
  Didn't faze Joe at all—
But evvytime he fired
  A cop would fall.

    The tear-gas made him laugh
      When they let it fly,
    Laughing gas made him hang
      His head an' cry.

He threw the hand grenades back
  With a outshoot drop,
An' evvytime he threw
  They was one less cop.

The Chief of Police said
    "What kinda *man* is this?"
And held up his shirt
    For a armistice.

"Stop gunning, black boy,
    And we'll let you go."
"I thank you very kindly,"
    Said my ole boy Joe.

            "We promise you safety
                If you'll leave us be—"
            Joe said: "That's agreeable
                Sir, by me . . . "

IV

The sun had gone down
    The air it was cool,
Joe stepped out on the pavement
    A fighting fool.

            Had walked from the jail
                About half a square,
            When a cop behind a post
                Let him have it fair.

Put a bullet in his left side
    And one in his thigh,
But Joe didn't lose
    His shootin' eye.

            Drew a cool bead
                On the cop's broad head;
            "I returns you yo' favor"
                And the cop fell dead.

The next to last words
    He was heard to speak,
Was just what you would look for
    From my boy Joe Meek.

        Spoke real polite
            To the folks standing by:
        "Would you please do me one kindness,
            Fo' I die?

"Won't be here much longer
    To bother you so,
Would you bring me a drink of water
    Fo' I go?"

        The very last words
            He was heard to say,
        Showed a different Joe talking
            In a different way.

"Ef my bullets weren't gone,
    An' my strength all spent—
I'd send the chief something
    With a compliment.

        "And we'd race to hell,
            And I'd best him there,
        Like I would of done here
            Ef he'd played me fair."

                V

So you cain't never tell
    How fas' a dog can run
When you see him a-sleeping,
    In the sun.

If you like this book . . . THE LAST RIDE OF WILD BILL
you will like some of our other books listed on the inside front
cover or on our flyers. You can order them conveniently by mail-
ing this order form.

I enclose $_____ for the books listed below.
(Add 25 cents for postage and handling.)

Author	Title	Price	No. of Copies	Total

Send me free subscription to Newsletter ☐

Send me free announcements of new books ☐

Postage and Handling _____.25

Grand Total $_____

Name_____

Address_____

City_____State_____Zip_____

Mail check or money order to
BROADSIDE PRESS
Dept. M.O., 12651 Old Mill Place   Detroit, Michigan 48238